PIANO • VOCAL • GUITAR

Passion HERE FOR YOU

ISBN 978-1-4584-0113-7

 sixstepsrecords

 Worship TOGETHER

HAL•LEONARD® CORPORATION

7777 W. BLUEMOUND RD. P.O. BOX 13819 MILWAUKEE, WI 53213

Visit Hal Leonard Online at
www.halleonard.com

Here for You

Words and Music by TIMOTHY WANSTALL,
MATT REDMAN, MATT MAHER
and JESSE REEVES

5

BREAKDOWN

CHORUS 2

Be wel-come in Your house, ___ Lord. ___

Be wel-come in Your house. ___

Chords Used in This Song

C   Fmaj⁹   F²   G   C/E   Dm⁷   G/B   Am⁷

Symphony

Words and Music by JASON INGRAM,
CHRIS TOMLIN, MATT REDMAN,
MATT MAHER and LOUIE GIGLIO

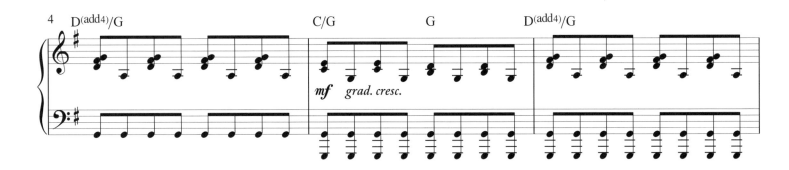

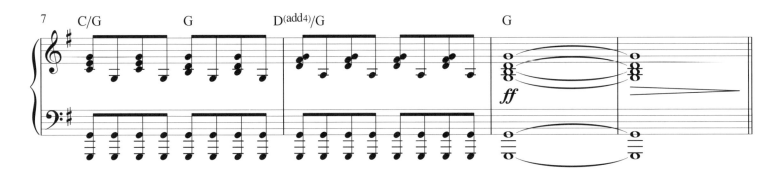

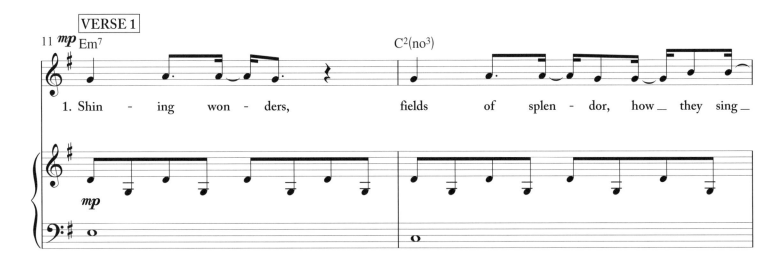

1. Shin - ing won - ders, fields of splen - dor, how _ they sing _

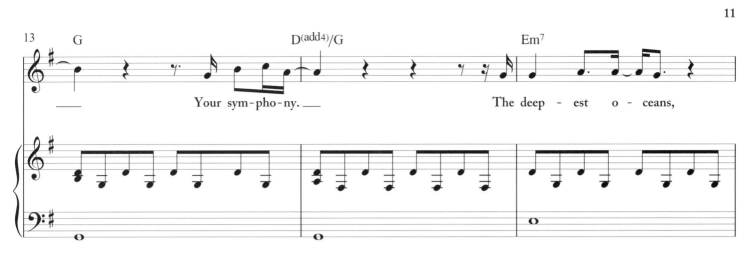

Your sym-pho-ny. ___ The deep - est o - ceans,

ris - ing moun - tains, how they ___ sing Your sym-pho-ny. ___

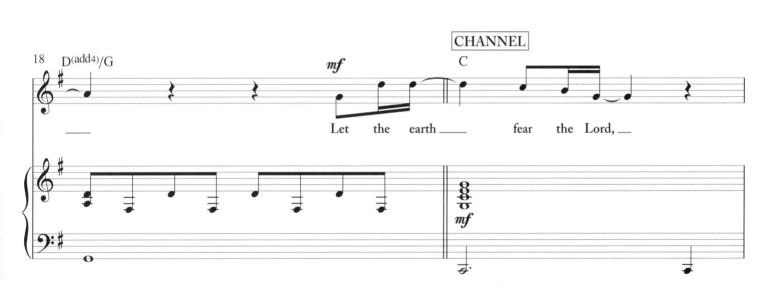

CHANNEL

Let the earth ___ fear the Lord, ___

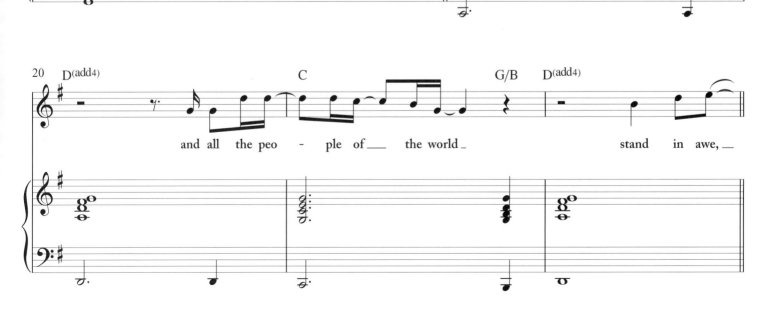

and all the peo - ple of ___ the world ___ stand in awe, ___

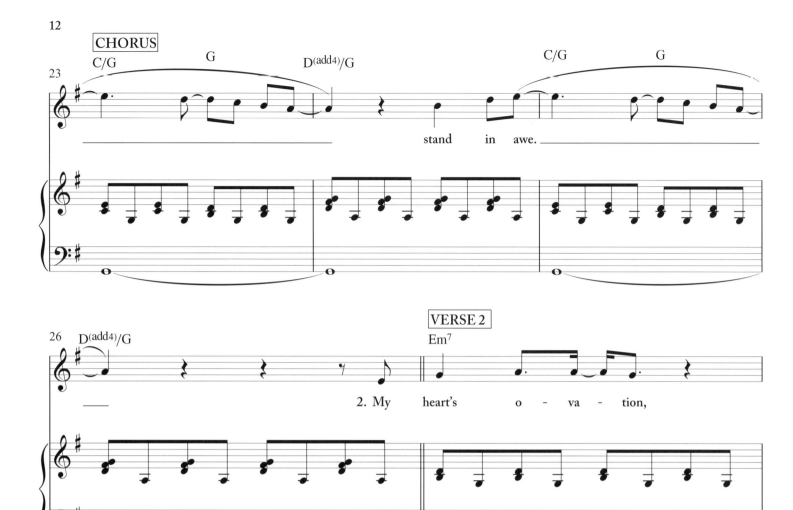

CHORUS

stand in awe.

VERSE 2

2. My heart's o - va - tion,

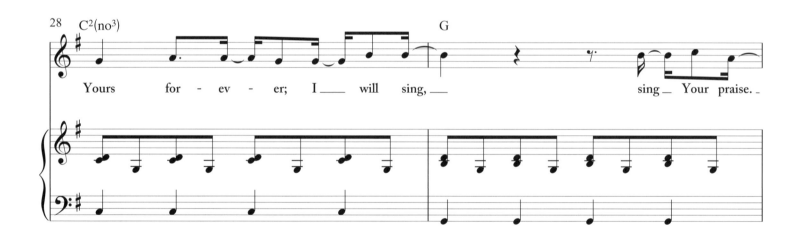

Yours for - ev - er; I __ will sing, __ sing __ Your praise.

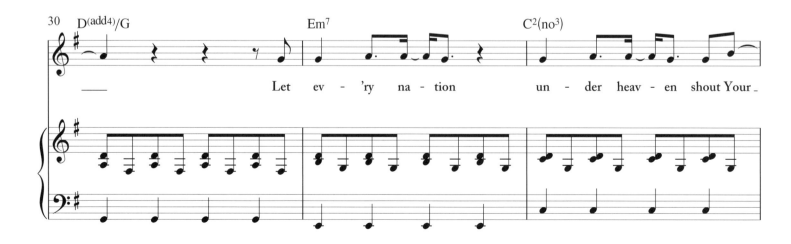

Let ev - 'ry na - tion un - der heav - en shout Your __

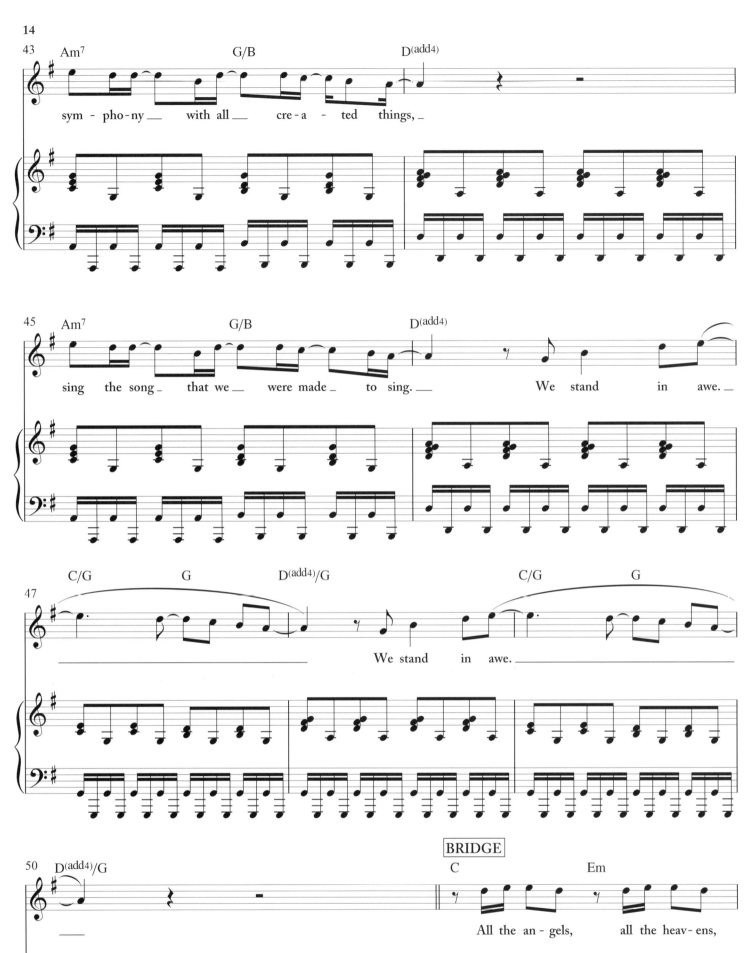

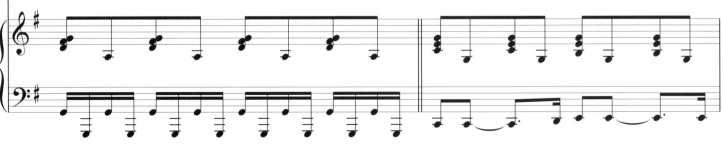

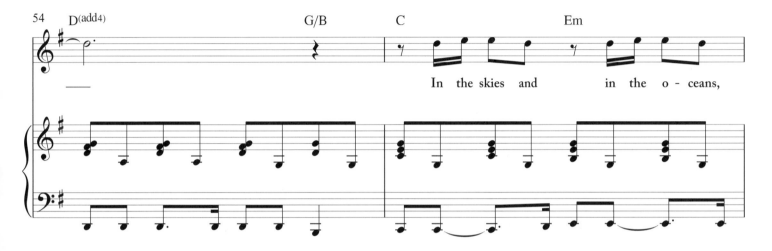

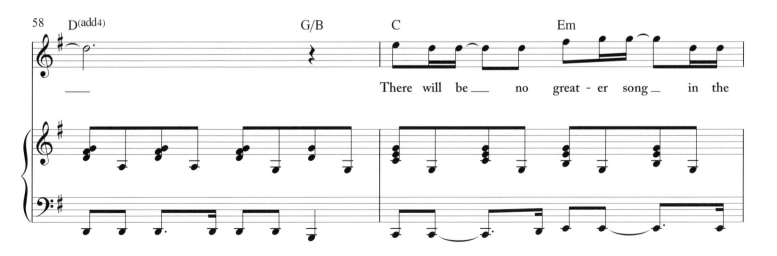

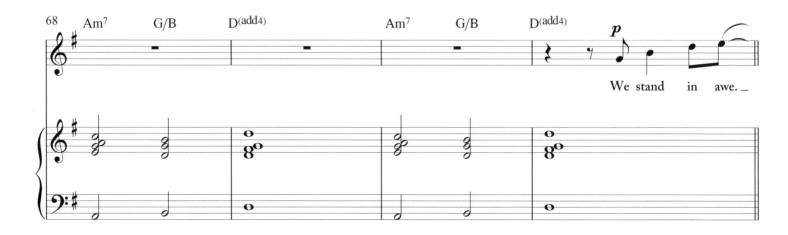

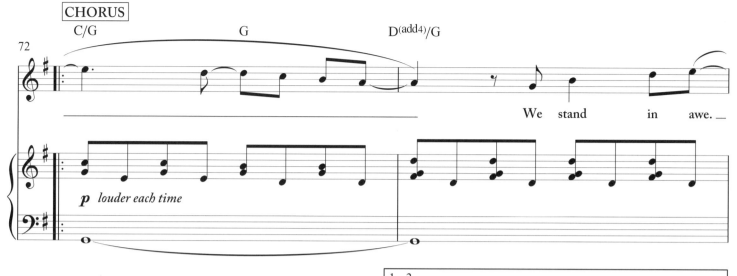

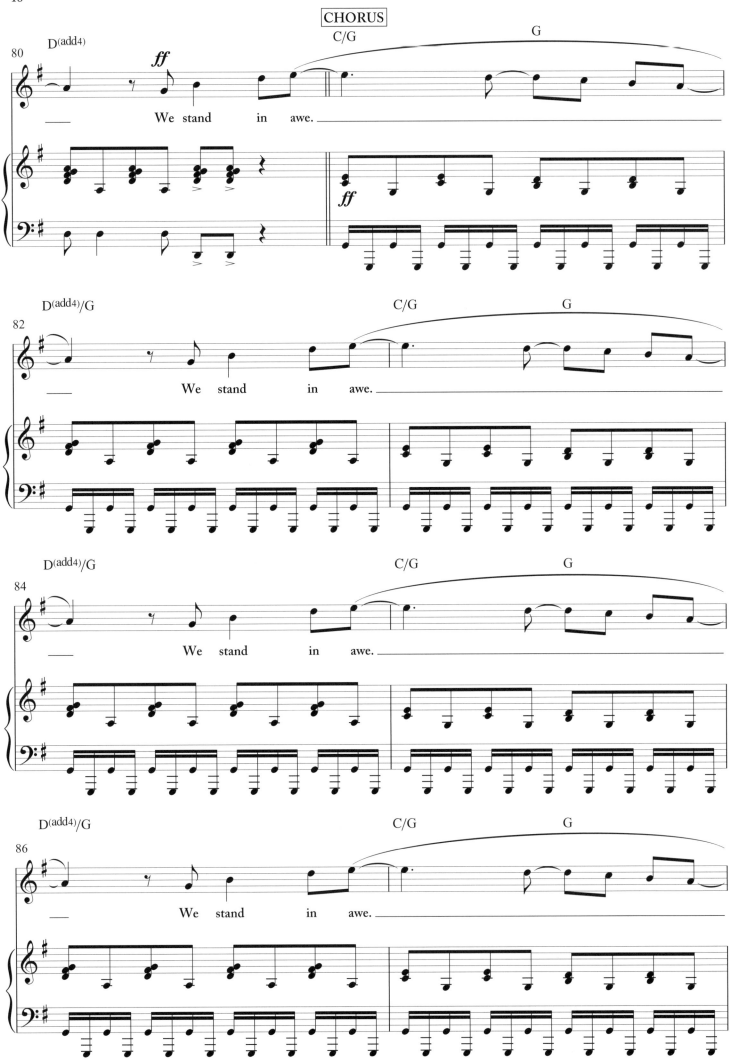

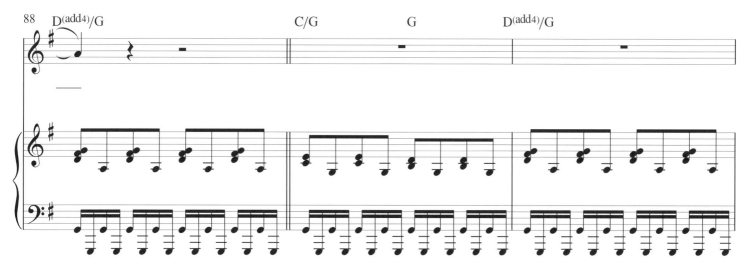

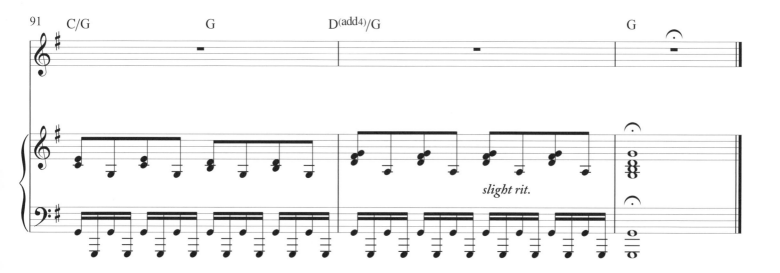

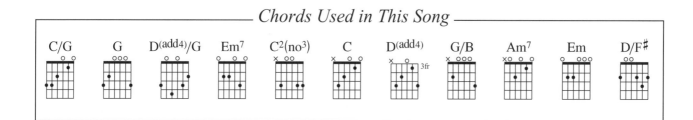

Chords Used in This Song

Waiting Here for You

Words and Music by CHRIS TOMLIN,
JESSE REEVES and MARTIN SMITH

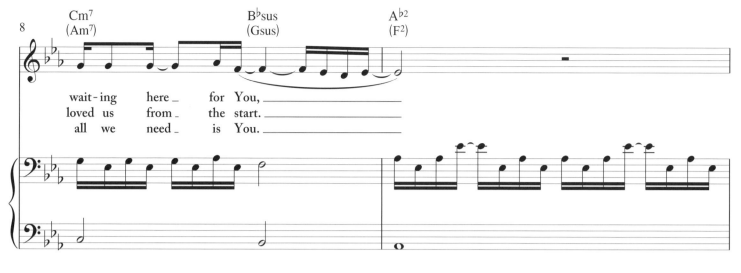

wait-ing here _ for You, _____
loved us from _ the start. _____
all we need _ is You. _____

wait-ing here _ for You. _____

2. You're the Lord _

Wait-ing here _ for You, _

CHORUS

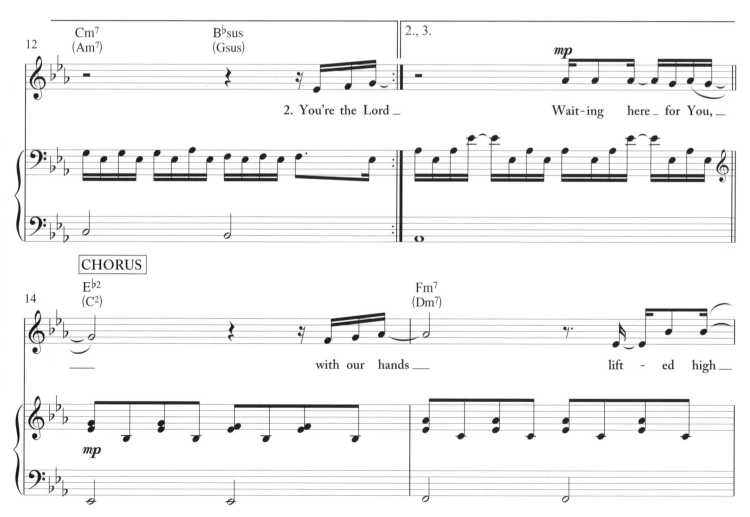

with our hands ___

lift - ed high _

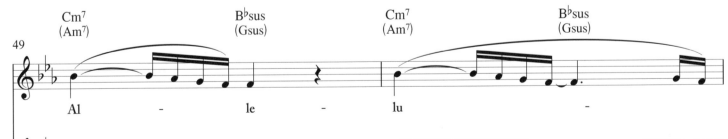

─ *Chords Used in This Song* ─

All My Fountains

Words and Music by CHRIS TOMLIN,
NATHAN NOCKELS, CHRISTY NOCKELS
and DANIEL CARSON

Strong acoustic rhythm ♩ = 105

VERSE 1

1. This dry and des-ert land, ___ I tell my - self, _ "Keep walk - ing on." _

Here's some - thing up a - head: _ wa - ter fall - ing like _ a

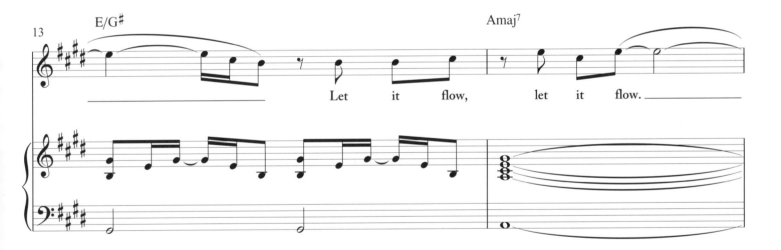

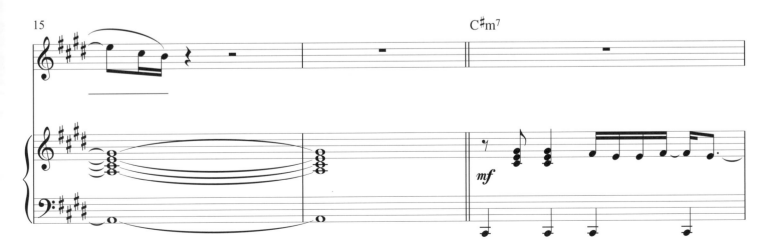

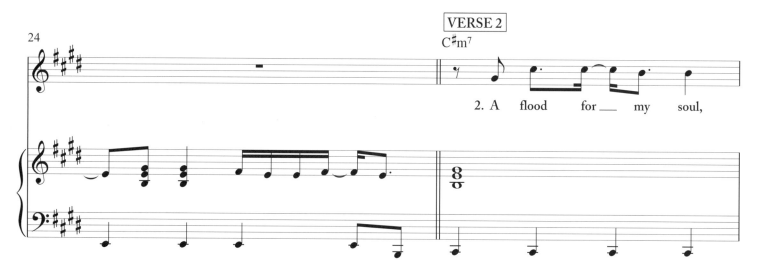

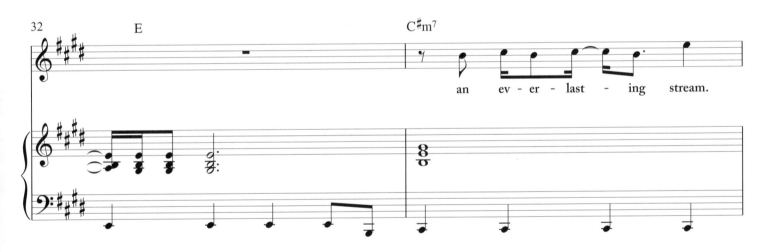

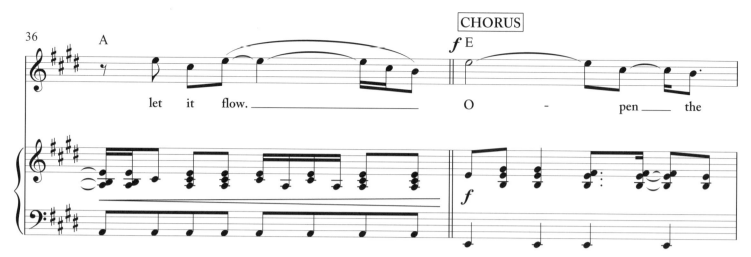

CHORUS

let it flow. _____ O - pen ___ the

heav - ens. __ Come, _____ liv - ing wa - ter. All ___ my

foun - tains __ are in ___ You. ___

You're strong _____ like ___ a riv - er, ___ Your

love ___ is run - ning _ through. All ___ my foun - tains _

INTERLUDE

are in ___ You. ___

Come on, _ and

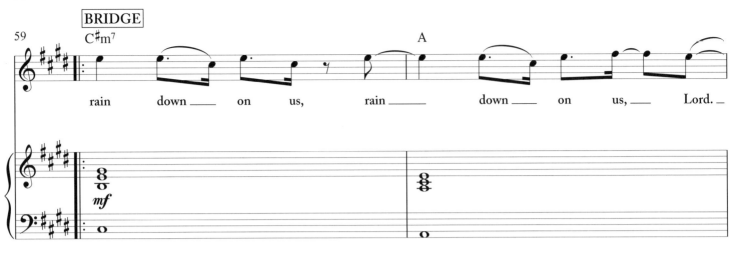

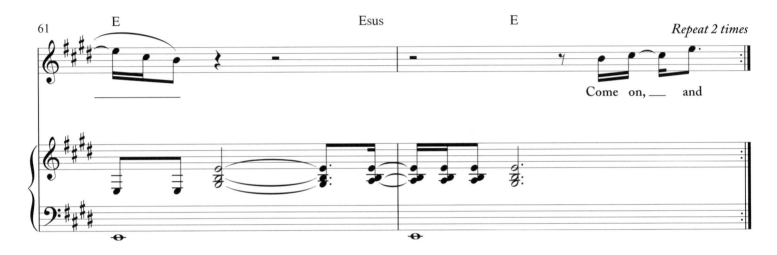

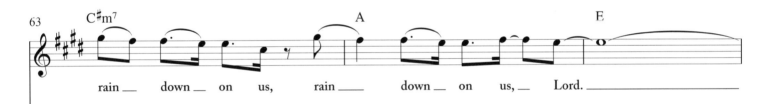

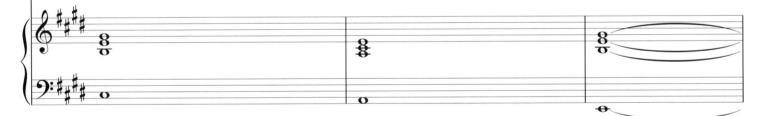

Come, _____ liv - ing wa - ter. All ___ my foun - tains __

are in ___ You! ___ You're

strong _____ like ___ a riv - er, ___ Your love is

run - ning _ through. All ___ my foun - tains _ are in ___ You. _

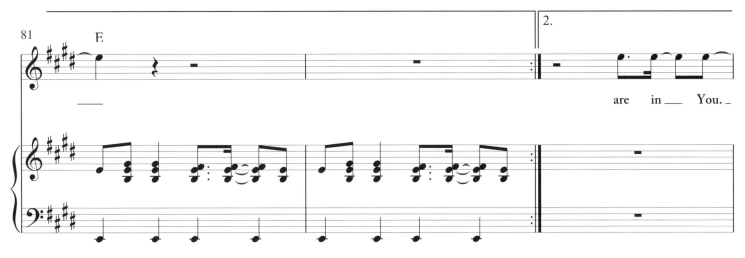

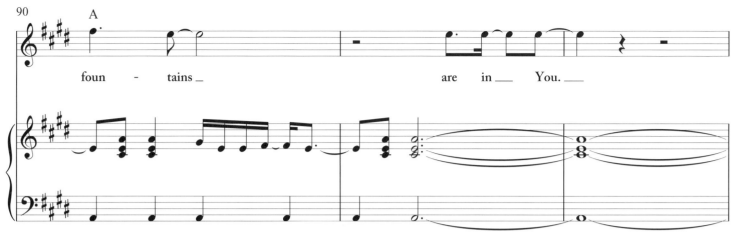

foun - tains ___ are in ___ You. ___

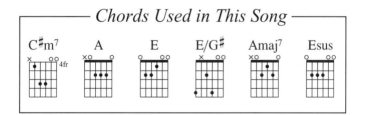

Chords Used in This Song

C#m7 A E E/G# Amaj7 Esus

Shadows

Words and Music by
DAVID CROWDER

And yet will __ He bring dark to __ light. __

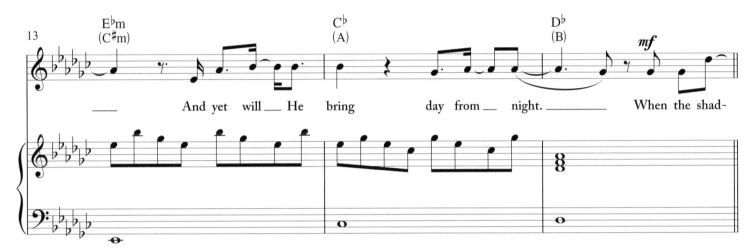

__ And yet will __ He bring day from __ night. _____ When the shad-

CHORUS

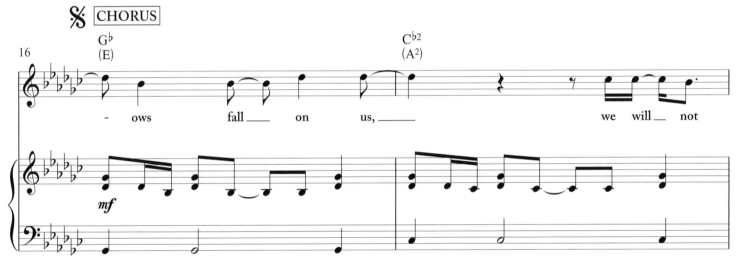

- ows fall __ on us, _____ we will __ not

fear; we will __ re - mem - ber. When

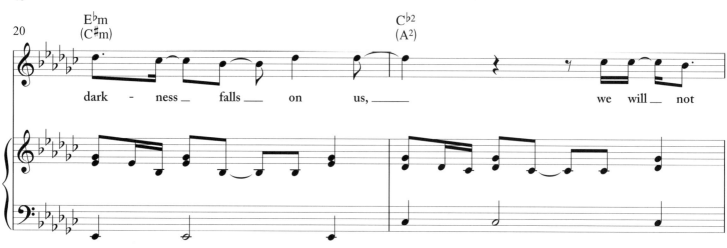

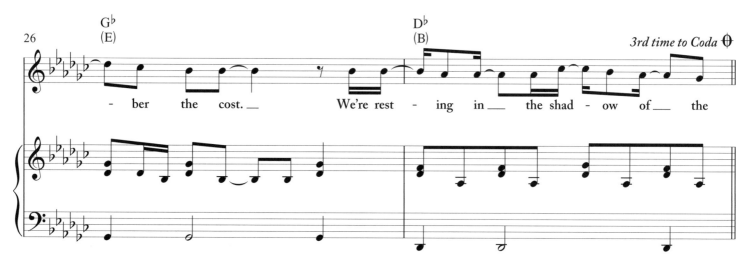

not count my life as an-y val-ue, pre-cious at all.   Let me fin-ish my race,   let me an-swer Your call.
When   the   shad -

D.S. al Coda

CODA

cross.

mp

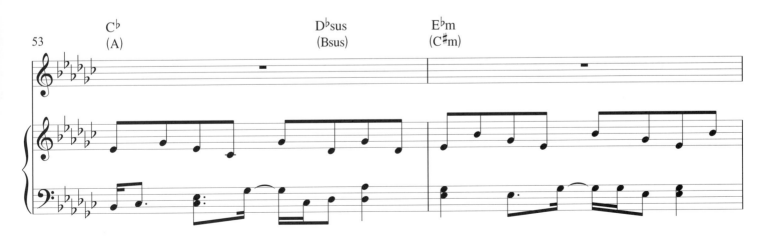

CHORUS

When the shad - ows fall ____ on us, ____

____ we will ____ not fear; we will ____ re - mem -

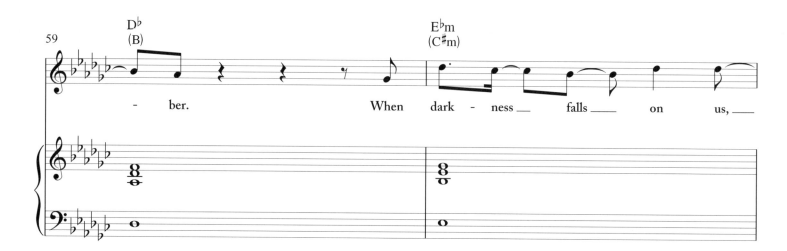

- ber. When dark - ness ____ falls ____ on us, ____

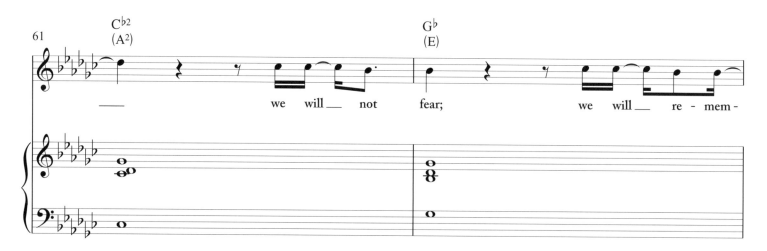

____ we will ____ not fear; we will ____ re - mem -

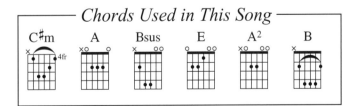

Lord, I Need You

Words and Music by JESSE REEVES,
KRISTIAN STANFILL, MATT MAHER,
CHRISTY NOCKELS and DANIEL CARSON

Capo 4 (G)

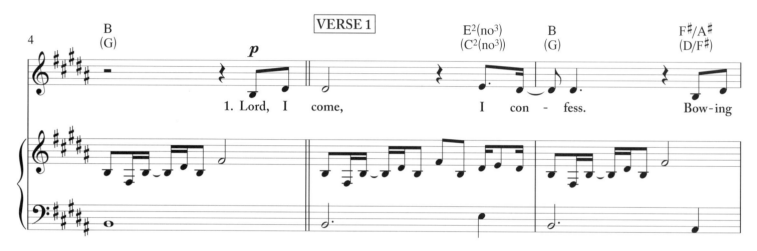

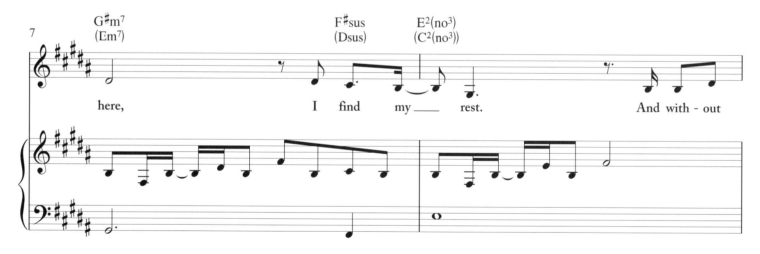

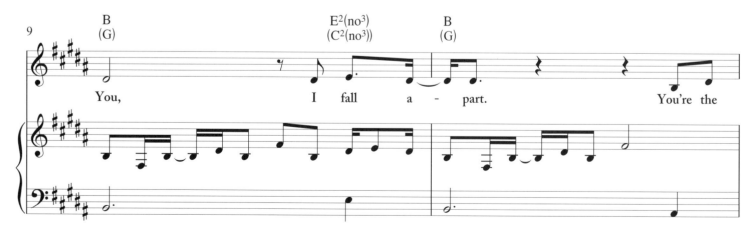

VERSE 2

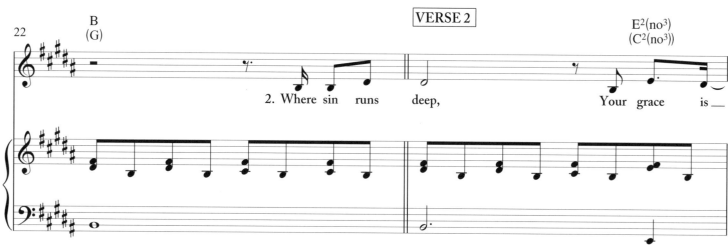

2. Where sin runs deep, Your grace is —

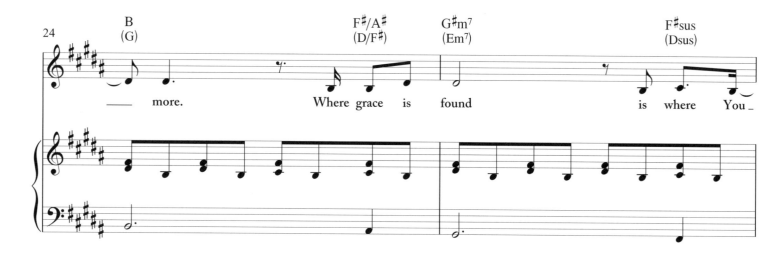

— more. Where grace is found is where You —

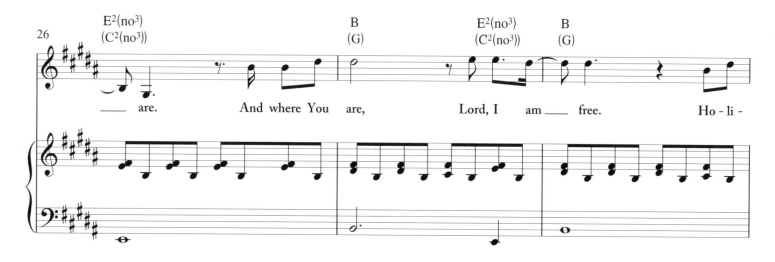

— are. And where You are, Lord, I am — free. Ho-li-

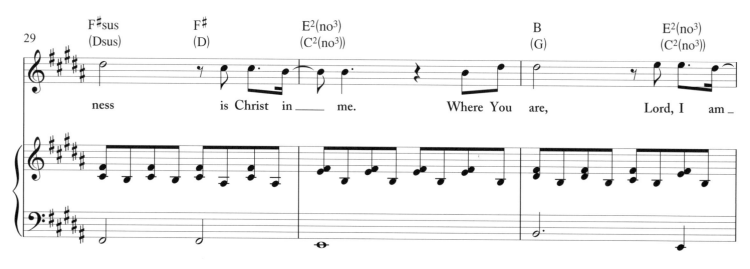

ness is Christ in — me. Where You are, Lord, I am —

BRIDGE

So teach my song to rise to You

when temp - ta - tion comes my way. And when I

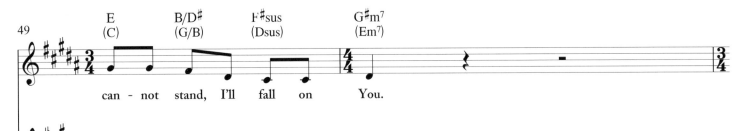

can - not stand, I'll fall on You.

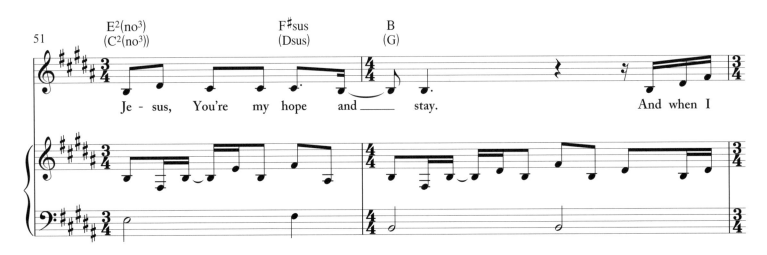

Je - sus, You're my hope and _____ stay. And when I

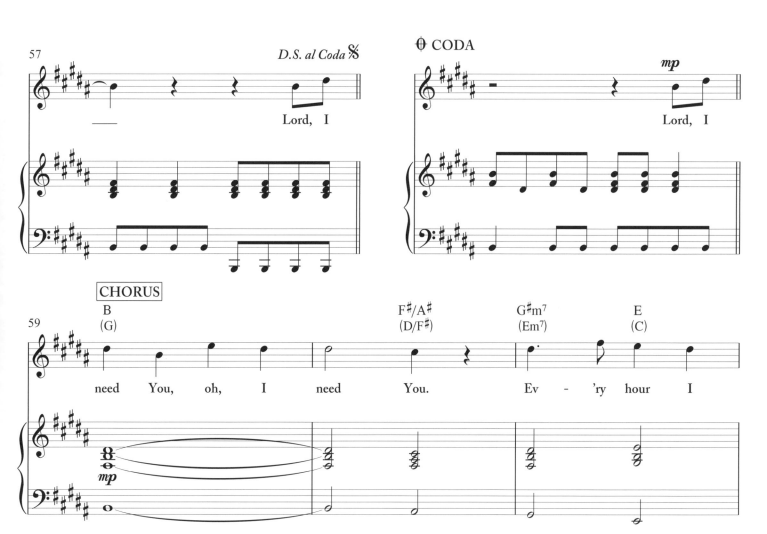

52

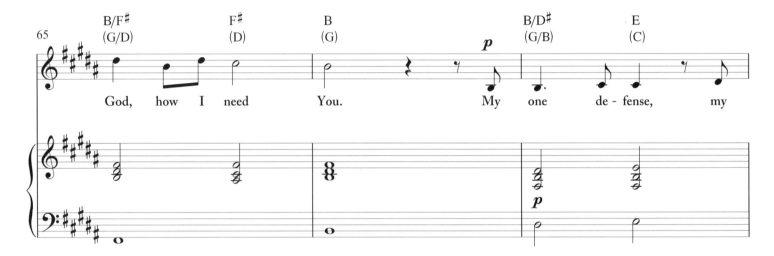

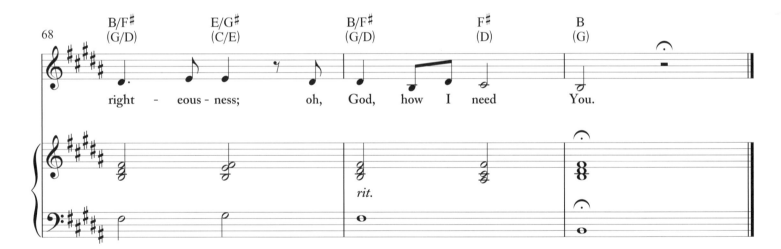

Chords Used in This Song

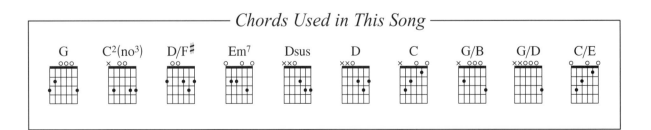

Set Free

Words and Music by JASON INGRAM,
CHRIS TOMLIN, MATT REDMAN
and BEN FIELDING

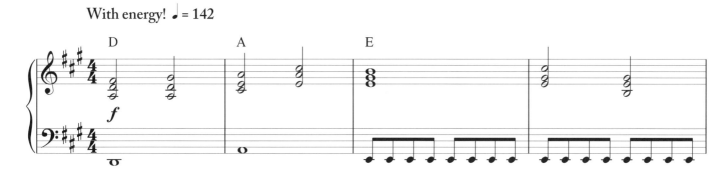

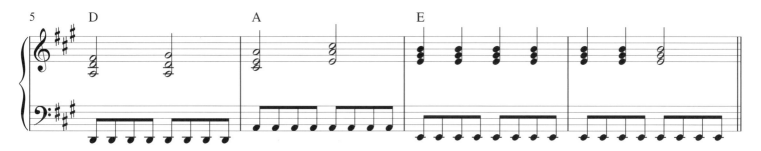

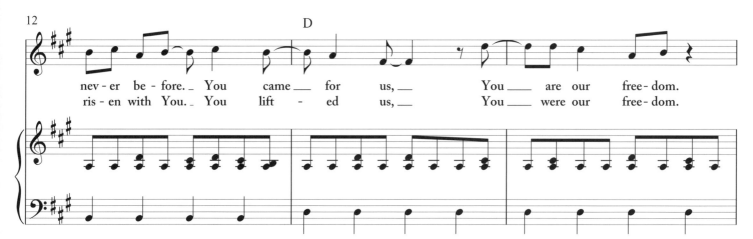

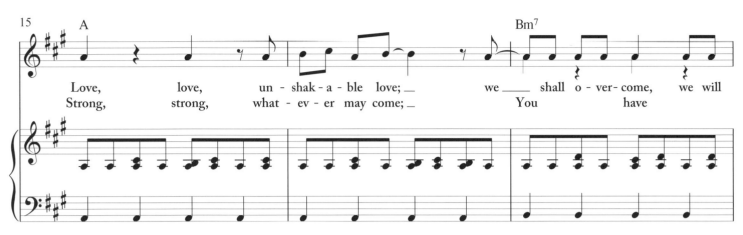

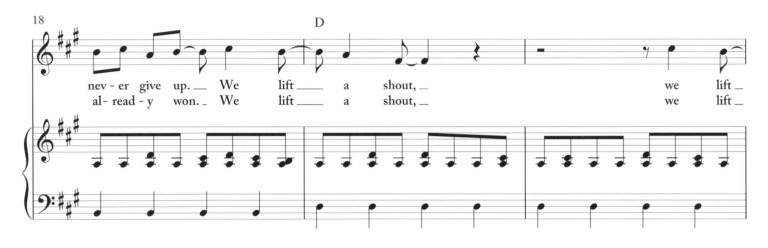

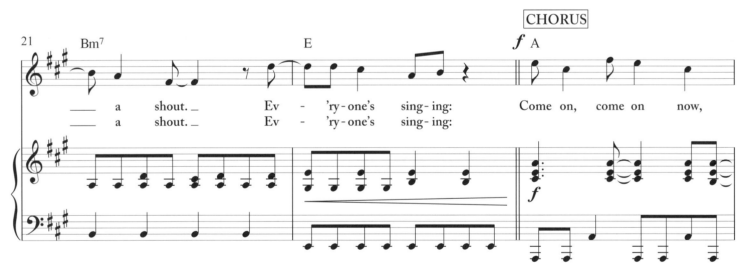

BRIDGE

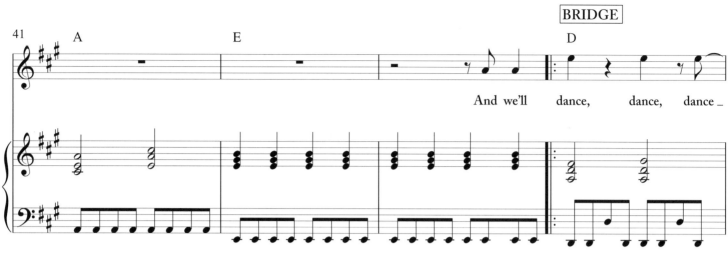

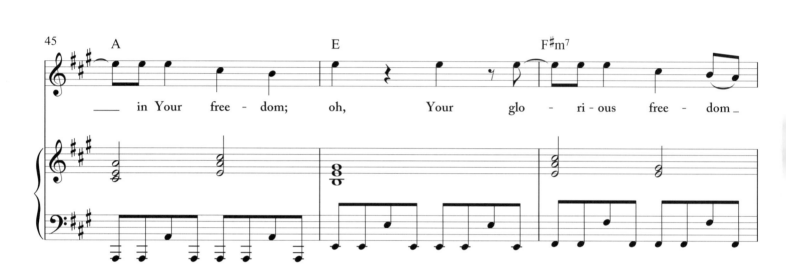

CHORUS

Come on, come on now, we've got a new song.

Come on, come on now, a song of lib-er-ty. Let the world hear

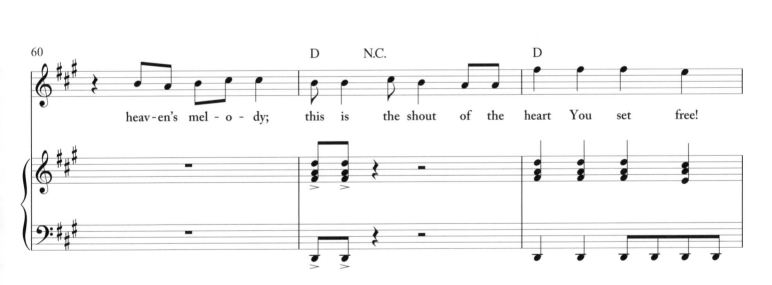

heav-en's mel-o-dy; this is the shout of the heart You set free!

Come on, come on now, we've got a new song. Come on, come on now,

a song of lib-er-ty. Let the world hear heav-en's mel-o-dy;

this is the shout of the heart You set free!

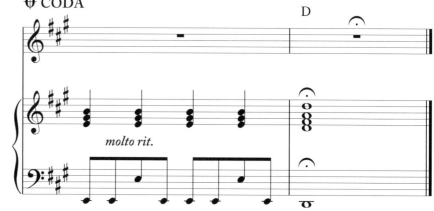

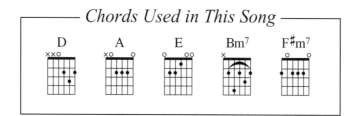

Chords Used in This Song

D   A   E   Bm⁷   F♯m⁷

Forever Reign

Words and Music by REUBEN MORGAN
and JASON INGRAM

60

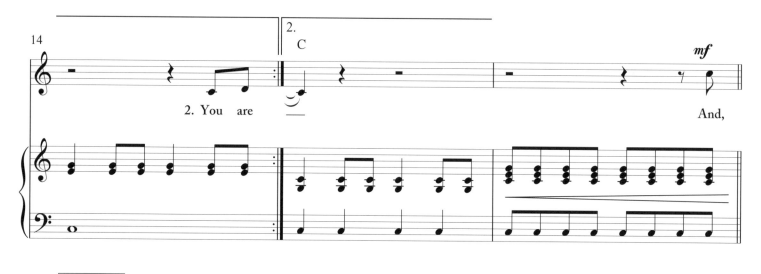

CHORUS

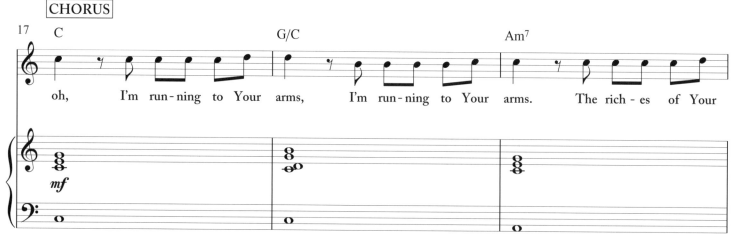

CHORUS

64

CHORUS

For - ev - er ___ reign. ___

My heart will sing ___ no oth - er name,

mp *gradual rit.*

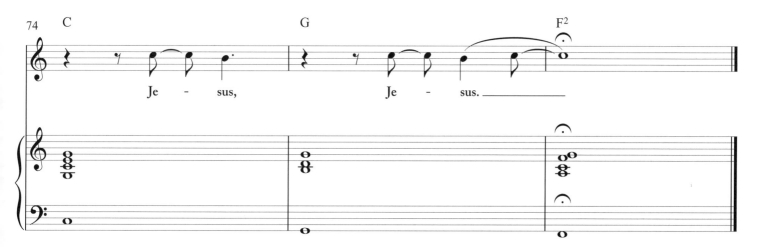

Je - sus, ___ Je - sus. ___

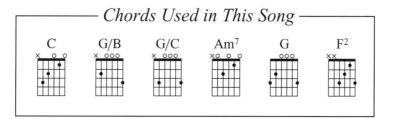

Chords Used in This Song

C   G/B   G/C   Am7   G   F2

Sometimes

Words and Music by
DAVID CROWDER

CHORUS 1

CODA

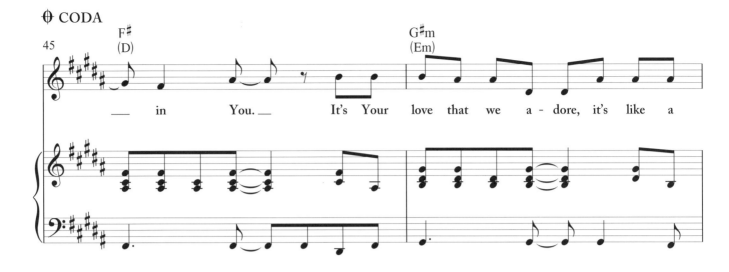

in You. __ It's Your love that we a - dore, it's like a

sea with - out a shore. We're lost __ in You, __ we're lost __ in You. __ It's Your

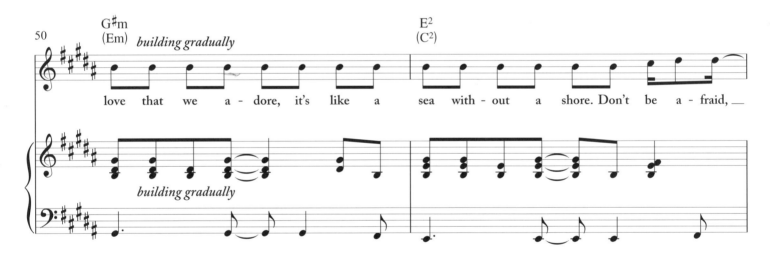

love that we a - dore, it's like a sea with - out a shore. Don't be a - fraid, __

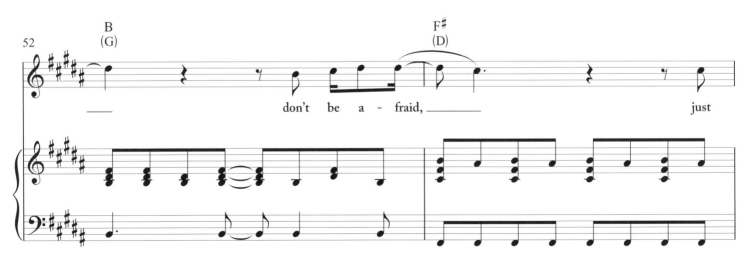

don't be a - fraid, _____ just

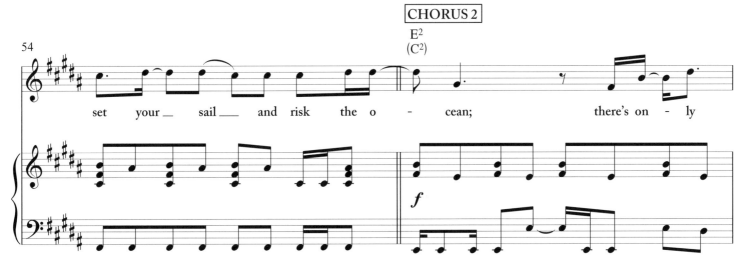

CHORUS 2

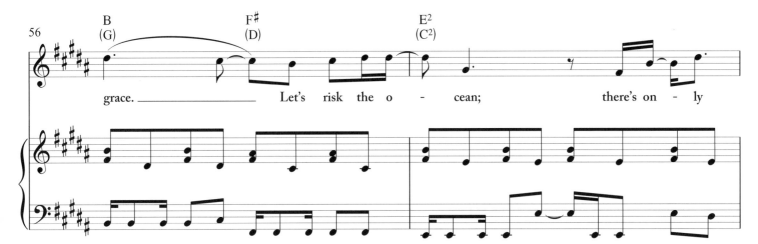

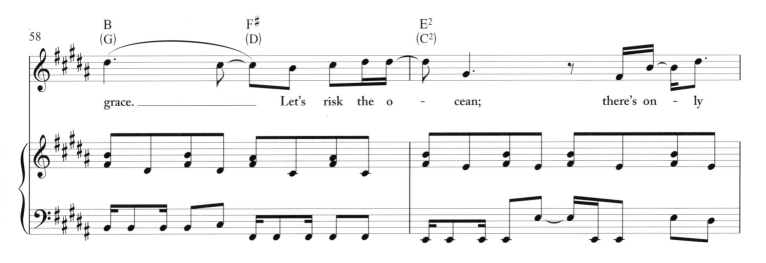

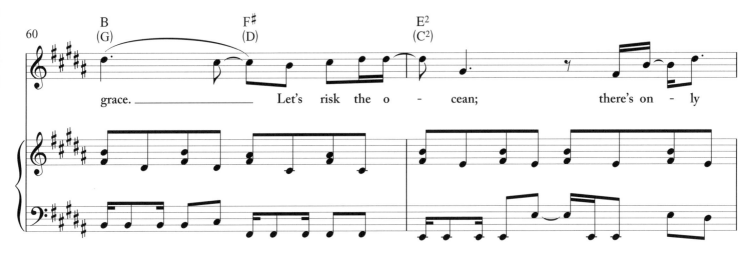

BRIDGE

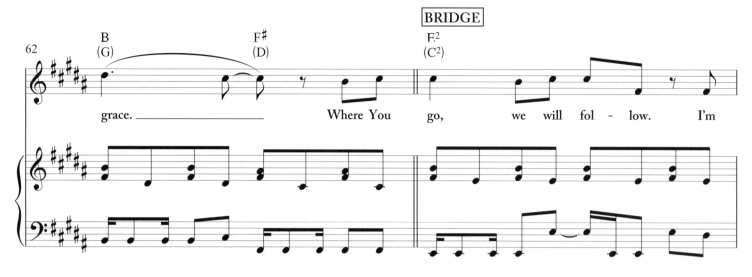

grace. _____ Where You go, we will fol - low. I'm

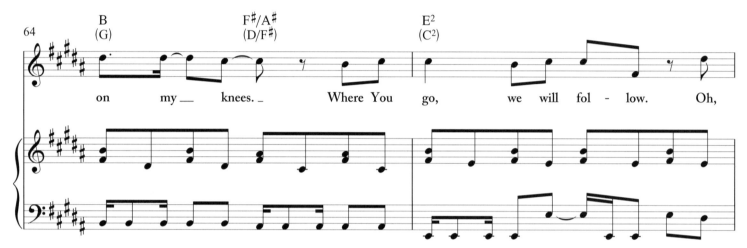

on my __ knees. __ Where You go, we will fol - low. Oh,

God, send __ me! Where You go, we will fol - low. I'm

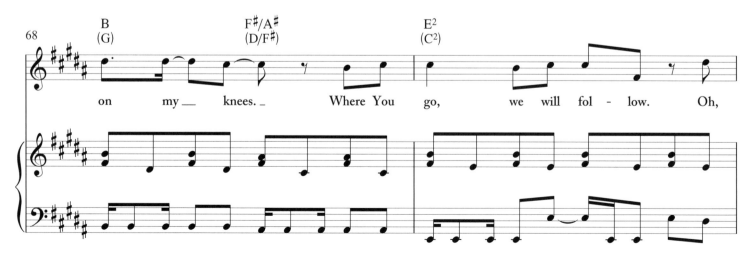

on my __ knees. __ Where You go, we will fol - low. Oh,

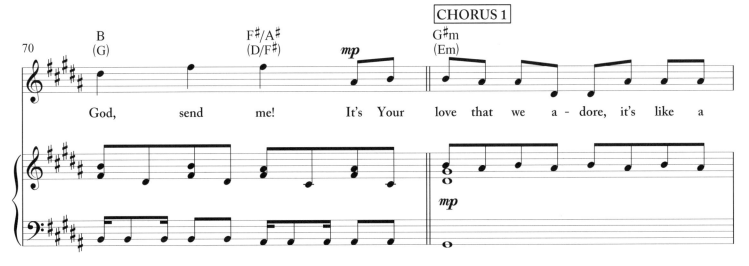

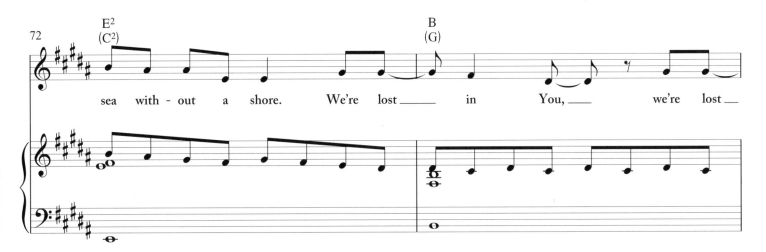

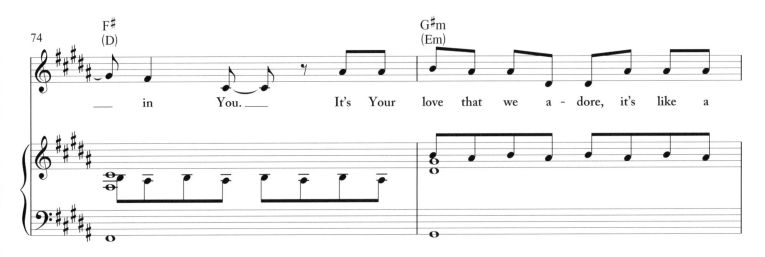

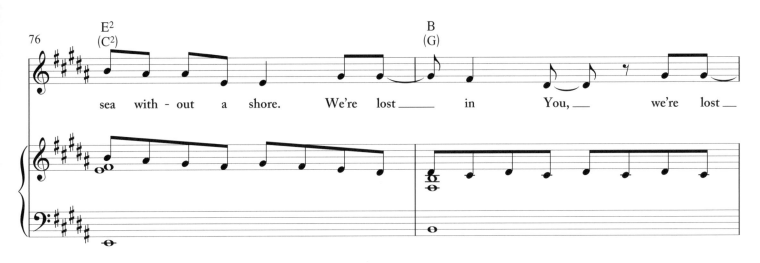

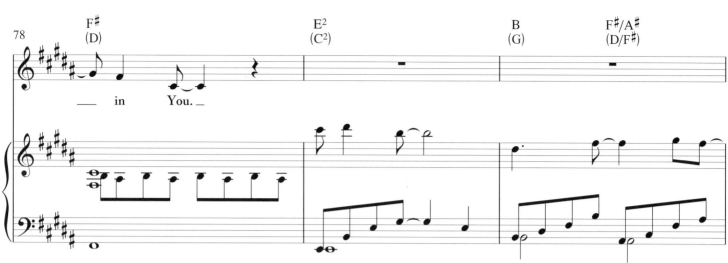

in You.

Where You go, we will fol-low.

Where You go, we will fol-low. Where You

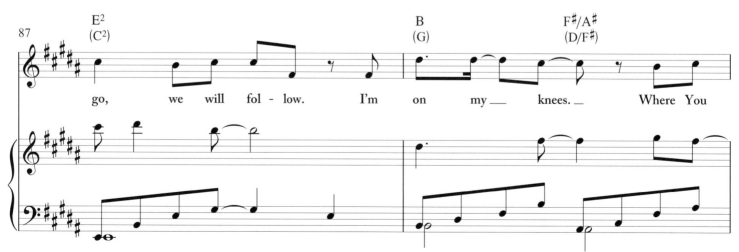

go, we will fol-low. I'm on my __ knees. __ Where You

go, we will fol-low. Oh, God, send me!

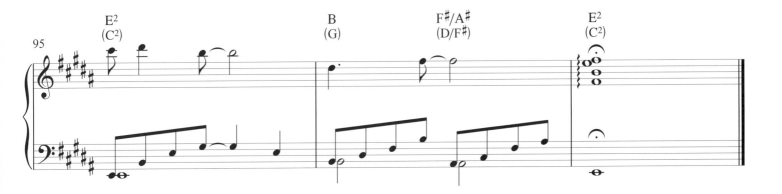

Chords Used in This Song

Always

Words and Music by JASON INGRAM
and KRISTIAN STANFILL

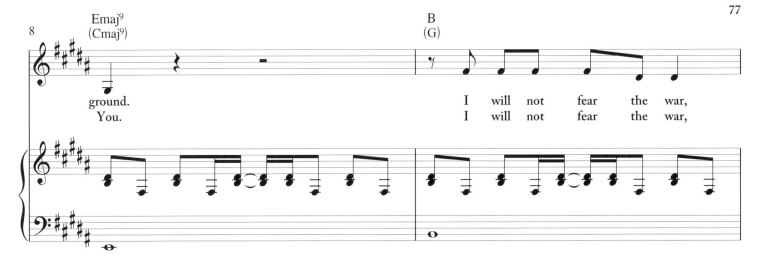

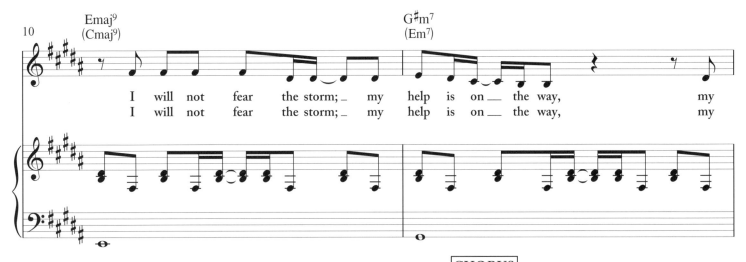

CHORUS

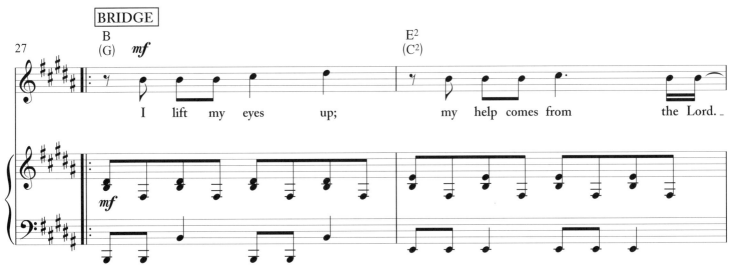

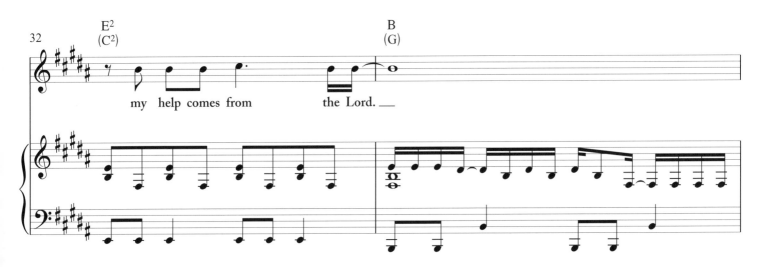

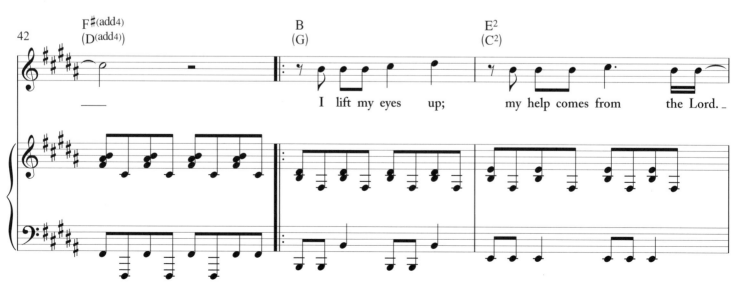

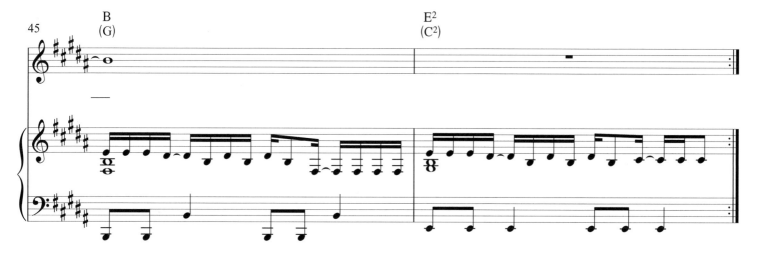

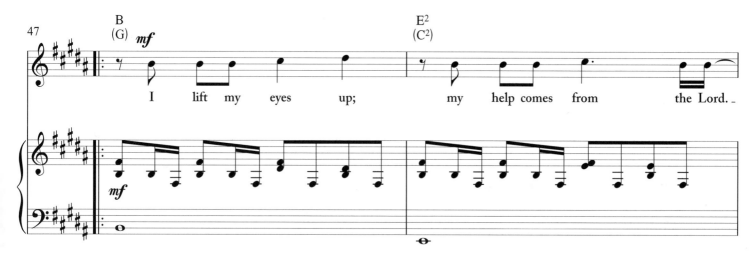

I lift my eyes up; my help comes from the Lord.

Repeat as desired

rit. last time

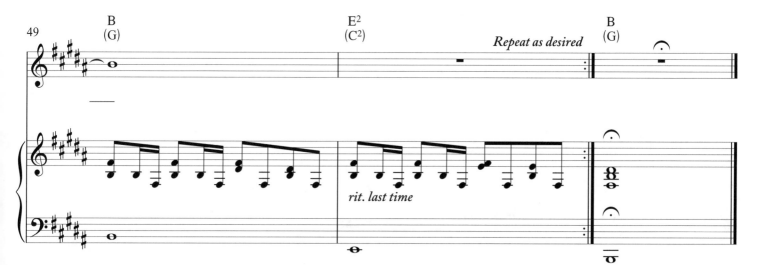

Chords Used in This Song

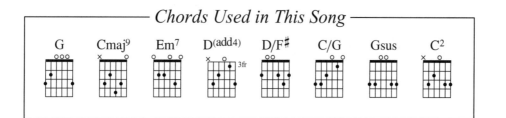

G   Cmaj⁹   Em⁷   D⁽ᵃᵈᵈ⁴⁾   D/F♯   C/G   Gsus   C²

Carry Your Name

Words and Music by JASON INGRAM,
CHRIS TOMLIN, NATHAN NOCKELS
and CHRISTY NOCKELS

84

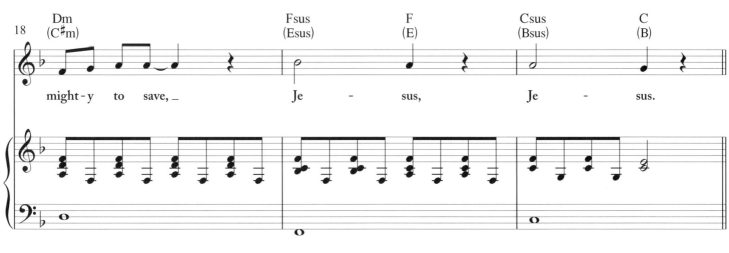

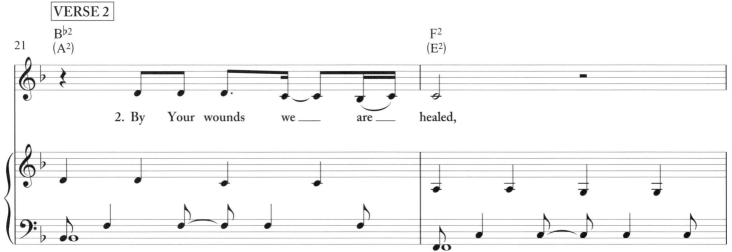

VERSE 2

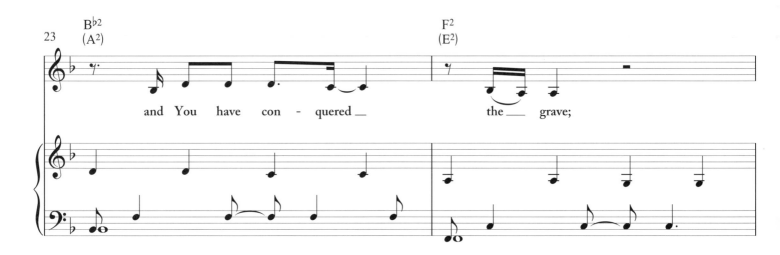

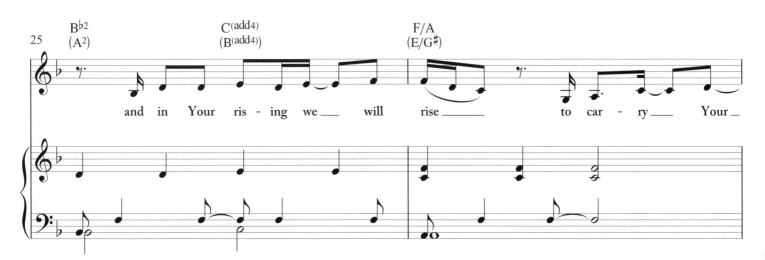

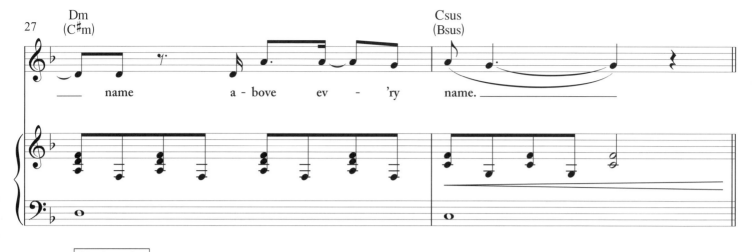

CHORUS 1

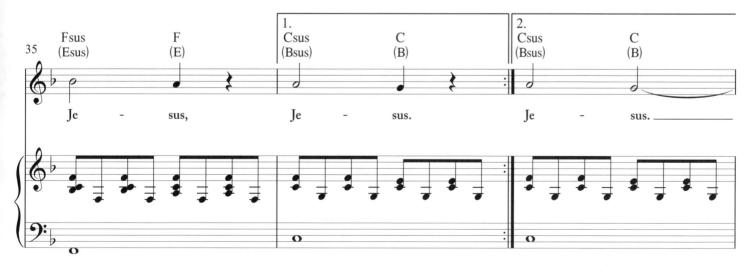

CHORUS 2

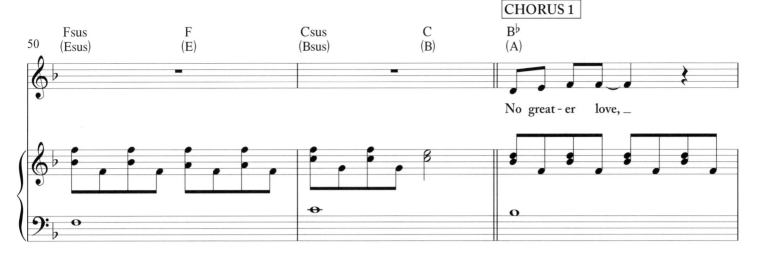

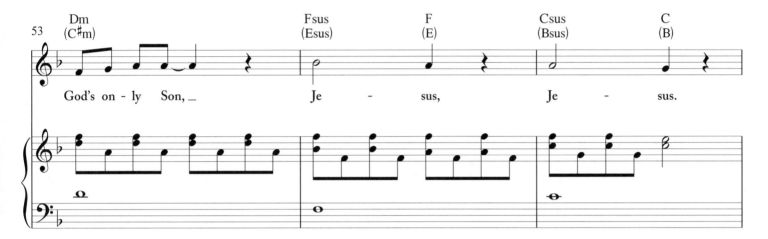

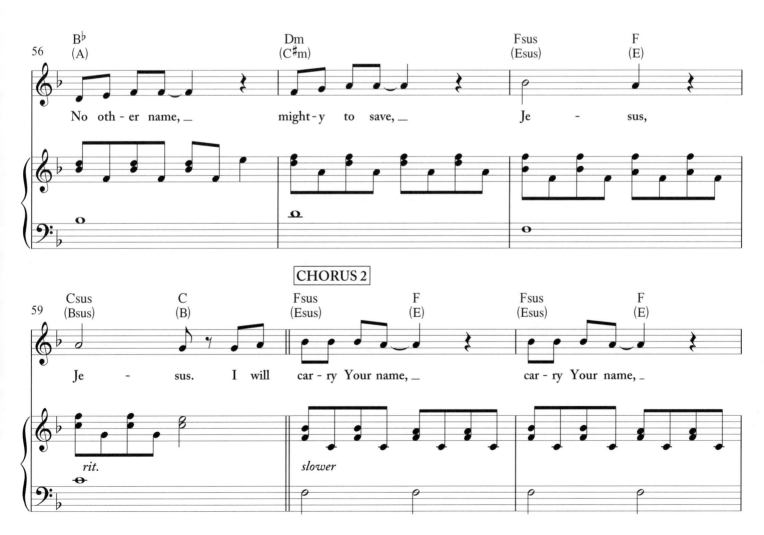

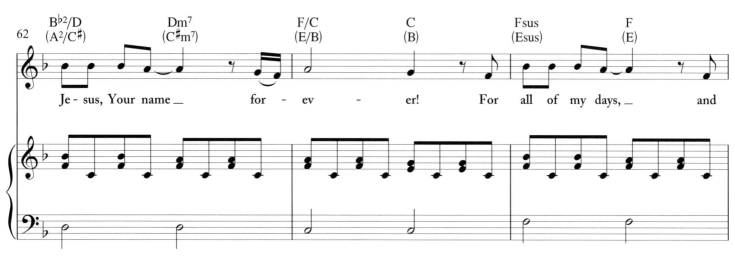

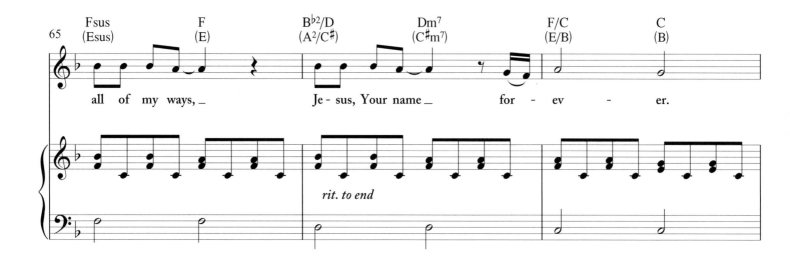

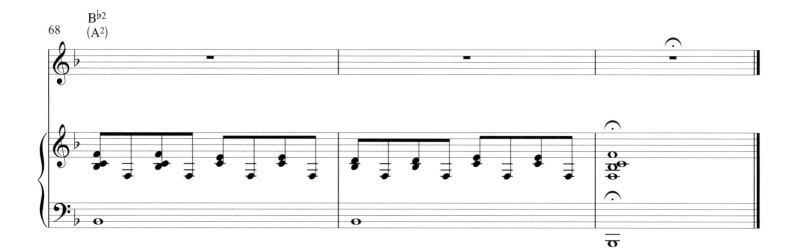

Chords Used in This Song

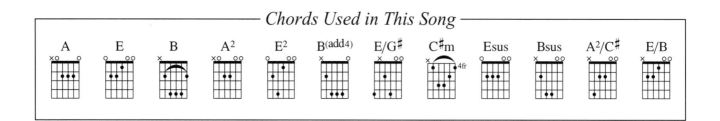

Spirit Fall

Words and Music by JASON INGRAM,
LOUIE GIGLIO, KRISTIAN STANFILL
and DANIEL CARSON

L.H. 8th notes 2nd time

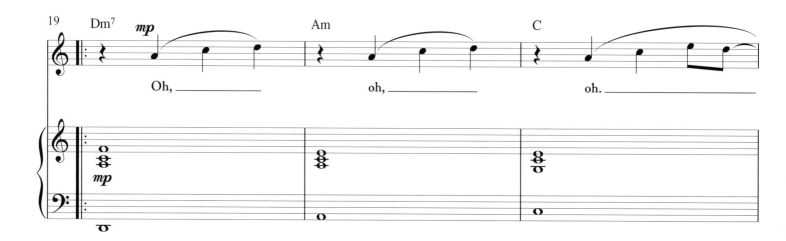

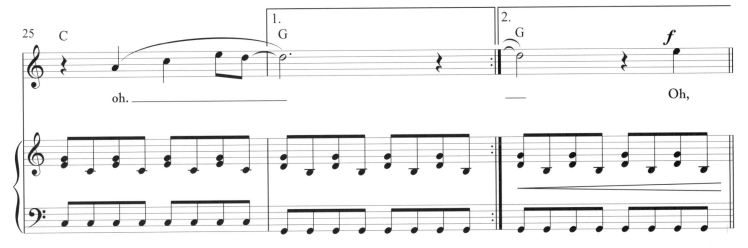

CHORUS 2

92

Son,   Sav - ior of ___ the world,   the hope   for

ev - 'ry - one.   Oh, _____   oh, _____

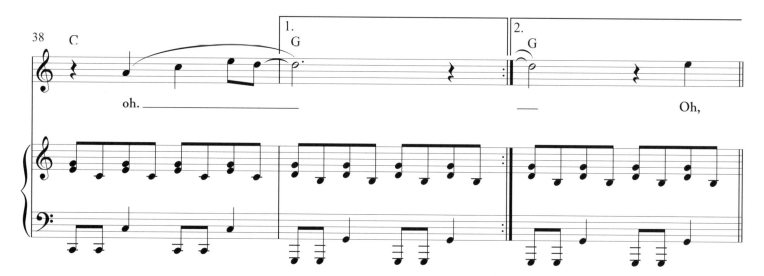

oh. _____   Oh,

come   mag - ni - fy ___ the   Son,   Sav - ior of ___ the

Drums only

Son, Sav - ior of ___ the world, the hope for ev - 'ry -

CHORUS 1

one. ___ Spir - it fall, Spir - it

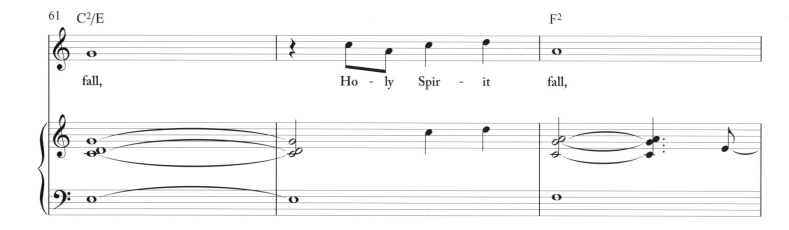

fall, Ho - ly Spir - it fall,

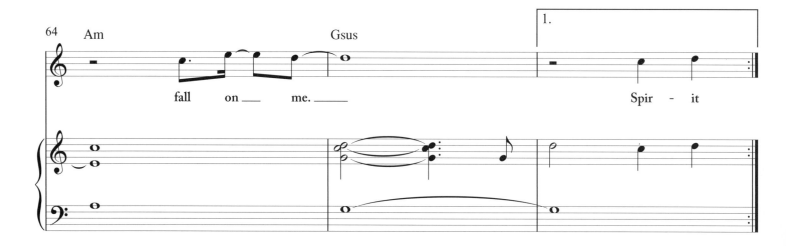

fall on ___ me. ___ Spir - it

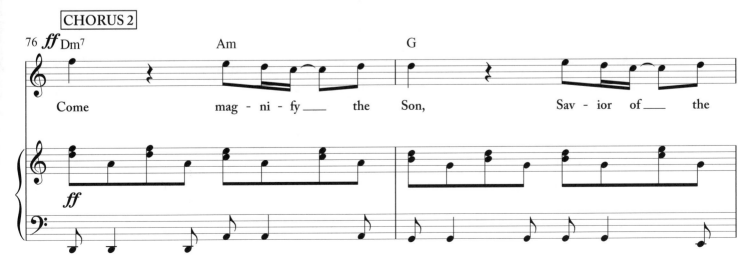

world, the hope for ev - 'ry - one. Oh, come mag - ni - fy ___ the

Son, Sav - ior of ___ the world, the hope for

ev - 'ry - one.

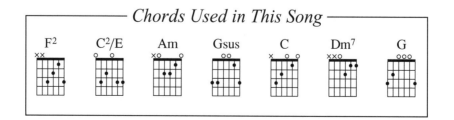

Chords Used in This Song